T0059712

*For Liv and Sven, the most evolved creatures
I know. With all my affection.*

Raphaël Martin

*To my parents and grandparents for their life
and their affection, and to Raymond Campan for
passing on his passion for evolution.*

Henri Cap

*To my mother for her tenderness
and perpetual help.*

Fred L.

*The authors would like to thank
Tony Voinchet for his investment in
this project.*

Copyright © 2022 by Schiffer Publishing, Ltd.

Translated from the French by Simulingua, Inc.

Originally published as *Évolutions* © 2020,
Saltimbanque Éditions

Library of Congress Control Number: 2021942594

All rights reserved. No part of this work may be
reproduced or used in any form or by any means—graphic,
electronic, or mechanical, including photocopying or
information storage and retrieval systems—without written
permission from the publisher.

The scanning, uploading, and distribution of this book or
any part thereof via the Internet or any other means without
the permission of the publisher is illegal and punishable
by law. Please purchase only authorized editions and do
not participate in or encourage the electronic piracy of
copyrighted materials.

"Schiffer Kids" logo is a trademark of Schiffer Publishing, Ltd.
Amelia logo is a trademark of Schiffer Publishing, Ltd.

Type set in Avenir LT Std

ISBN: 978-0-7643-6386-3
Printed in India

Published by Schiffer Kids
An imprint of Schiffer Publishing, Ltd.
4880 Lower Valley Road
Atglen, PA 19310
Phone: (610) 593-1777; Fax: (610) 593-2002
Email: Info@schifferbooks.com
Web: www.schifferbooks.com

For our complete selection of fine books on this and
related subjects, please visit our website at www.
schifferbooks.com. You may also write for a free catalog.

Schiffer Publishing's titles are available at special
discounts for bulk purchases for sales promotions or
premiums. Special editions, including personalized
covers, corporate imprints, and excerpts, can be
created in large quantities for special needs. For more
information, contact the publisher.

EVOLUTIONS

Raphaël Martin and Henri Cap

Illustrations by Fred L.

Schiffer**Kids**

4880 Lower Valley Road, Atglen, PA 19310

OVERVIEW

Where do our eyes come from? What about our lungs—did we inherit them from ancient fish? Why do we look so much like certain monkeys? To unravel these mysteries, follow our two curious friends back in time. They will take you along the path of evolution, a natural process of change that began hundreds of millions of years ago. It explains how human beings and all living things came to be. Here are the topics that we will explore.

THE ORIGINS OF THE WORLD

Atoms   Page 10

THE BEGINNINGS OF LIFE

Molecules   Page 12

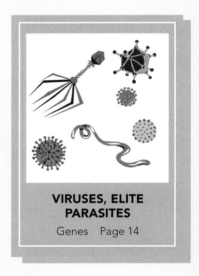

VIRUSES, ELITE PARASITES

Genes   Page 14

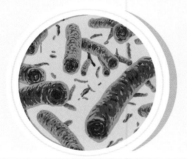

THE TIME OF ARCHAEA AND BACTERIA

The First Cells   Page 16

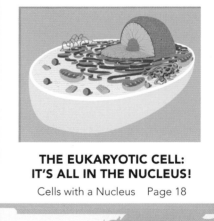

THE EUKARYOTIC CELL: IT'S ALL IN THE NUCLEUS!

Cells with a Nucleus   Page 18

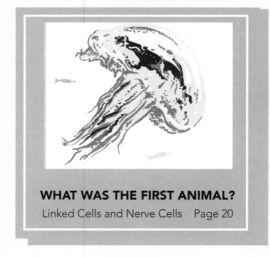

WHAT WAS THE FIRST ANIMAL?

Linked Cells and Nerve Cells   Page 20

WHAT IS A LIVING BEING?

Fungi, plants, bacteria, and animals, including humans, are all living things. These organisms are made up of one or more cells, which produce energy and substances that are essential to life. In each cell, there is a molecule called DNA. The genes in DNA contain the information needed for the cell to function and reproduce.

PRIMATES ENTER THE SCENE
Opposable Thumbs and
3-D Vision   Page 28

THE ARRIVAL OF SKELETONS
The Spinal Column   Page 22

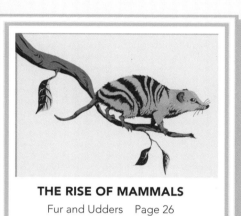

THE RISE OF MAMMALS
Fur and Udders   Page 26

STANDING TALL
Bipedalism   Page 30

**TETRAPODS AND THE
CONQUEST OF DRY LAND**
Arms and Legs   Page 24

While reading this book, you may see words that are new to you. You will find their definitions in the **GLOSSARY** on pages 36 and 37.

DID YOU SAY EVOLUTION?

Ancient Greek poets thought that a god named Prometheus created the first human out of land and water. Today, some people believe that plants, people, and animals were made by a divine being and have never evolved; others think that evolution is magical. In this book, we let scientists explain how life on earth came to be.

ADAPTATION . . .

In 1809, a French biologist named Jean-Baptiste Lamarck proposed that living things transform to survive in their environment. He reasoned that this need to adapt would produce a change in their bodies. For example, because giraffes must stretch to reach leaves on high branches, they developed long necks and legs to survive.

OR NATURAL SELECTION?

Fifty years later, the English naturalist Charles Darwin put forth a theory of natural selection. He said that individuals in a species are naturally different, and some have differences that are better suited to their environment. So, giraffes that have the longest necks are more likely to survive and reproduce than those with shorter necks.

WHAT DOES SCIENCE SAY?

When a living thing reproduces, its DNA can sometimes undergo changes by chance. If these changes are helpful to its survival, the creature will reproduce more easily than creatures without this trait. In addition, its offspring will have this advantage and continue to pass it on. One point for Darwin!

Although Lamarck's views have been disproven, he may have been a little bit right. Cells do activate or deactivate their genes according to signals sent by the environment (food, climate, and so on). This allows the body to adapt faster. Offspring can inherit these adaptations. One point (sort of) for Lamarck!

THE ORIGINS OF THE WORLD

The Big Bang was a huge explosion that gave birth to the universe 13.7 billion years ago. Since then, space has continued to expand. Stars, planets, and other celestial bodies are constantly forming, including the Earth, which is about 4.5 billion years old. The Big Bang is also at the origin of atoms, which are the smallest particles of all matter, whether nonliving or living things—including you!

OXYGEN AND HYDROGEN

These two atoms form the molecule for water: H_2O. Water has been present on Earth for 4.4 million years. An adult is made up of 65 percent water!

CARBON

This atom is part of the composition of sugars that serve as fuel for living beings. Together with calcium (another atom), it strengthens the bones of skeletons.

NITROGEN

This atom, along with oxygen, makes up the air that we breathe.

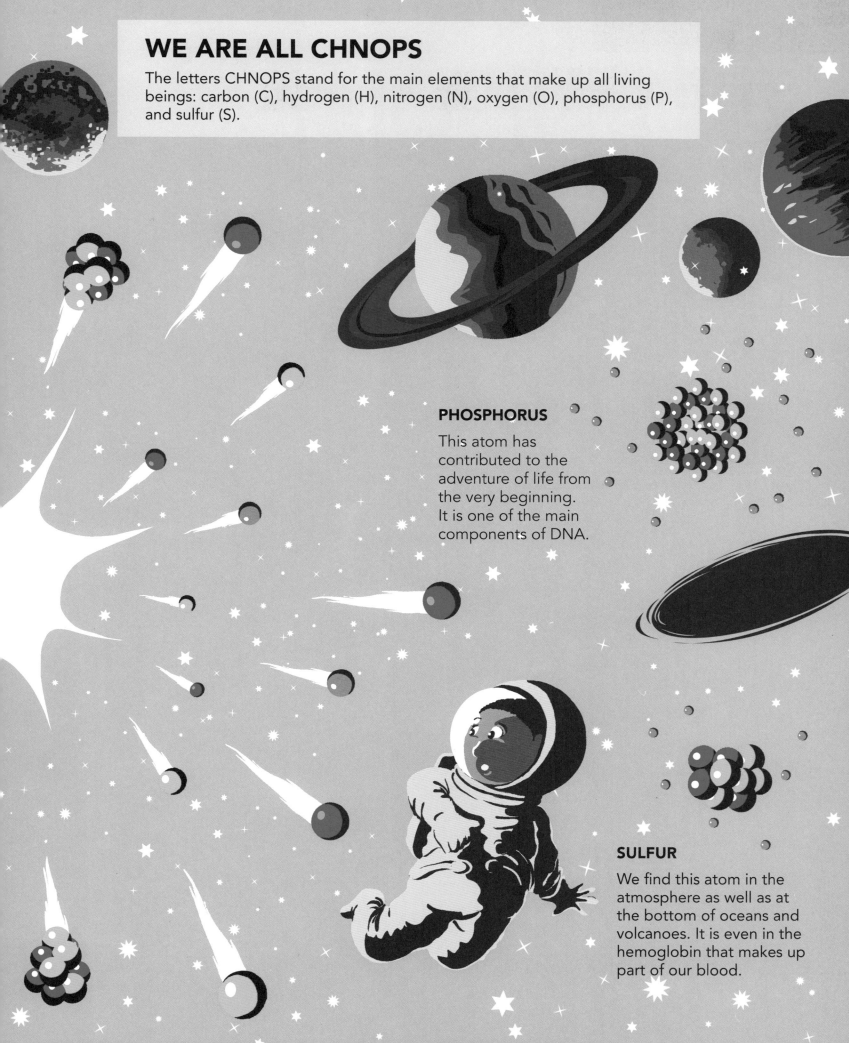

WE ARE ALL CHNOPS

The letters CHNOPS stand for the main elements that make up all living beings: carbon (C), hydrogen (H), nitrogen (N), oxygen (O), phosphorus (P), and sulfur (S).

PHOSPHORUS

This atom has contributed to the adventure of life from the very beginning. It is one of the main components of DNA.

SULFUR

We find this atom in the atmosphere as well as at the bottom of oceans and volcanoes. It is even in the hemoglobin that makes up part of our blood.

ATOMS, ELEMENTS, AND MOLECULES

Atoms are what elements are made of. There are 118 elements, including carbon, oxygen, nitrogen, iron, calcium, and sodium. Each element is made up of one type of atom. So, the carbon element is made up of only carbon atoms. Atoms have the ability to join together to form molecules. Some molecules are essential for living organisms, especially water, sugars, fats, and proteins.

THE BEGINNINGS OF LIFE

About 3.8 billion years ago, the Earth was like a big chemistry laboratory: the molecules present in the water of the oceans—agitated by the energy of the sun, lightning, and meteorites—interacted with each other. Scientists think this is likely when life appeared!

A MATTER OF BUBBLES

The first microscopic living beings may have formed at the edge of the oceans. Viewed through a magnifying glass, the foam of waves resembles moss. Like soapy water, it contains tiny bubbles, which could be at the origin of the protective membranes of these earliest beings. Another possibility is that life may have hatched near "black smokers," a kind of underwater volcano. We still find ancient microorganisms called archaea near these deep-sea vents.

LUCA, A COMMON ANCESTOR?

All living organisms today might have the same ancestor. Was it a simple molecule carrying a few genes? Was it more like a microscopic soap bubble? Scientists do not know yet, but they have called it LUCA, which stands for Last Universal Common Ancestor.

A SOUP FULL OF LIFE

In 1953, Stanley Miller, an American scientist, mixed water with a solution of chemicals that were present in Earth's atmosphere nearly four billion years ago. He zapped the mixture with an electrical charge to simulate lightning.

A week later, the mixture contained amino acids, molecules that are present in all living organisms. His "chemical soup" did not exactly reproduce the conditions when life appeared on Earth, but it surely has a taste of truth . . .

VIRUSES, ELITE PARASITES

Viruses have been part of the history of life for billions of years. Their specialty? They live on cells a thousand times bigger than themselves in order to reproduce.

▲
The flu, chicken pox, colds, and COVID-19 are all diseases that are transmitted by viruses. These membrane-equipped parasites have found a highly effective way to reproduce. By injecting their genes into a cell, they reprogram it to make millions of other viruses. A true infection!

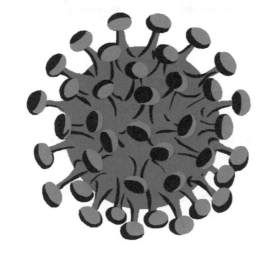

IT'S ALL IN THE GENES

Viruses use DNA to infect organisms. DNA is a molecule that is found inside the cells of almost all living things. It is what genes are made of, and it is passed down from parents to their offspring. These inherited genetic traits explain why family members resemble one another.

Baby elephants, like human babies, develop in their mother's womb thanks to a placenta. Most mammals no longer lay eggs, which are easily devoured by predators. ▼

GENE DONORS

Scientists believe that some of our human DNA comes from viruses. Why don't mammals, which are the cousins of lizards or turtles, lay eggs too? It's because a virus modified their DNA a long time ago and made them able to make the placenta, an organ that feeds an embryo in the womb.

THE TIME OF ARCHAEA AND BACTERIA

Originating in the oceans more than three billion years ago, archaea and bacteria were the first living things to populate our planet.

Some bacteria cause diseases (plague, tetanus, etc.). Others are indispensable, such as the ones that live in our digestive tract and help us with digestion. We swallow bacteria all the time, and in large quantities: a single gram of yogurt contains up to 10 million of them!

BACTERIA, FULL OF LIFE!

With the membrane that surrounds them, bacteria look like microscopic bags. Inside, a necklace-shaped DNA molecule carries the entire program needed for them to work and, more important, to allow them to reproduce. Present since the dawn of time, these microorganisms continue to populate continents and oceans.

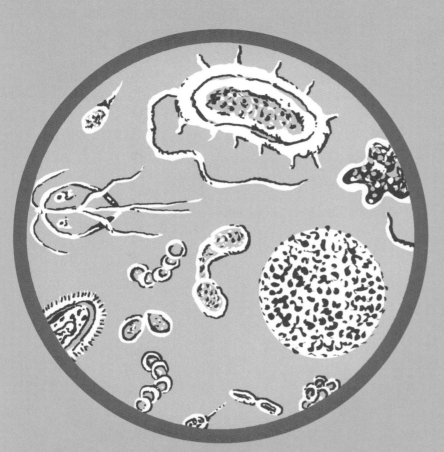

THE ANCESTORS OF OUR CELLS?

Bacteria and archaea are the oldest cells. They are made up of a DNA molecule, which is bathed in a gel, the cytoplasm, and is surrounded by a membrane. Their great advantage, compared to viruses, is their ability to live and reproduce without needing to exploit another organism. The cells that make up our body are probably the result of the long transformation of the first bacteria.

◄ Archaea live in extreme environments: frozen seas, salty lakes, hot geysers . . . even the human belly button! The most-resistant ones can withstand temperatures over 200°F. They are found near black smokers, the volcano-like vents that roar at the bottom of the oceans. It might be there that life was born!

ARCHAEA, CREATURES OF THE EXTREME

Archaea are the cousins of bacteria. What is one of the main differences between them? Their membranes are more resistant, which allows them to survive in almost any environment. Since their appearance three billion years ago, they have become a great help to humans. Present in our gut, with bacteria, they help with our digestion.

THE EUKARYOTIC CELL: IT'S ALL IN THE NUCLEUS!

About two billion years ago, a new kind of cells appeared: eukaryotic cells. These were more evolved than bacteria because they had a nucleus—a true control center. They could also assemble to form an organism. Each one had a specialized mission: reproduction, digestion, protection. They are what make up the human body!

ENLARGED BY 100,000

EVOLUTION THROUGH . . . INDIGESTION!

The first eukaryotic cells fed on bacteria. Some bacteria were poorly digested and continued to live inside the cells. Today, these ancient bacteria participate in the functions of animal and vegetable eukaryotic cells. That is the case, for example, with mitochondria, which are like tiny energy power plants. It's thanks to them that our muscles can function and our cells can breathe!

DNA is a succession of genes, which are chemical codes that program our cells to produce what we need to live. In bacteria, DNA is shaped like a necklace. In eukaryotic cells, this molecule is twisted on itself and enclosed in a nucleus. If we unfolded a human's DNA, it would be over 6 feet long!

▼

REPRODUCTION: TWO METHODS

A bacterium reproduces identically by dividing in two, a bit like photocopying. By contrast, some eukaryotic cells are capable of sexual reproduction. This method makes it possible to mix the genes of two individuals of the same species: a male and a female. Over generations of reproduction, the species adapts more quickly to its environment and therefore evolves faster.

SUPER-SPECIALIZED

Billions of eukaryotic cells make up the human body. The majority have a nucleus, and they all have a membrane. But their shape is different depending on their function. Some make up the muscles, some make up the blood, and some make hair or nails. Each one has its specialty!

A VISIT TO A CELL

 Nucleus: the command center

 Endoplasmic reticulum: where proteins are manufactured

 Mitochondria: power plants that produce energy

 Golgi device: stores fats and proteins

 Microtubules: tubes that serve as a skeleton for the cell

 Vesicles: carry the products manufactured by the cell

19

WHAT WAS THE FIRST ANIMAL?

Animals appeared almost 700 million years ago when clusters of cells joined together with a kind of natural glue. But what did they look like? Among the first were sponges, and then jellyfish, which still populate our oceans.

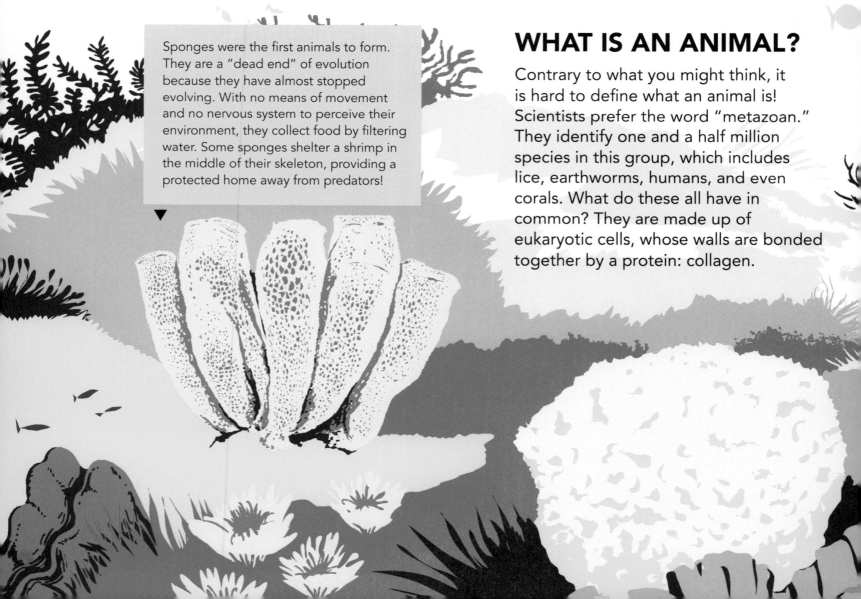

Sponges were the first animals to form. They are a "dead end" of evolution because they have almost stopped evolving. With no means of movement and no nervous system to perceive their environment, they collect food by filtering water. Some sponges shelter a shrimp in the middle of their skeleton, providing a protected home away from predators!

▼

WHAT IS AN ANIMAL?

Contrary to what you might think, it is hard to define what an animal is! Scientists prefer the word "metazoan." They identify one and a half million species in this group, which includes lice, earthworms, humans, and even corals. What do these all have in common? They are made up of eukaryotic cells, whose walls are bonded together by a protein: collagen.

A COMPLEX ORGANIZATION

Bacteria can cohabitate in groups without transforming. Animal cells can organize themselves into tissues and specialize. Some specialize in reproduction; others specialize in digestion, protection, or perception. For example, some jellyfish have eyes to perceive light. But unlike octopuses, they do not have a brain that would allow them to decipher the forms that surround them.

The first animals, such as jellyfish, corals, and sea anemones, were already equipped with specialized cells. They have highly sensitive sensors that trigger tiny poisonous "harpoons." Swimmers, beware! These prickly ancestors still wander the oceans.

THE ARRIVAL OF SKELETONS

About 550 million years ago, animals developed a way to protect their nervous system. This change marked the appearance of vertebrates, a family that today includes more than 50,000 species, including sharks, shrews, and humans!

COUSINS OF STARFISH

From the first animals, two lineages evolved separately. On one side were arthropods (crustaceans, insects), mollusks, and worms. Their nervous system is in a ventral (abdominal) position. On the other side were echinoderms (starfish, sea urchins) and the first fishlike vertebrates; their nervous system is in the dorsal position (spinal cord).

Vertebrates, such as humans and camels, have an internal skeleton that strengthens their bodies and allows them to perform many movements. By contrast, crabs, ladybugs, and snails have an external skeleton that is not very mobile, such as a carapace, cuticle, or shell.

INVENTION OF THE SKELETON

What were the first vertebrates? They were ancient kinds of fish that had a brain that was protected by a skull made of cartilage. They also had vertebrae organized in columns to protect their spinal cord. Their fins were equipped with muscles, which allowed them to move faster and to steer themselves. The lamprey, an ancient lineage of jawless fish, is still roaming the waters of oceans and rivers. It is a living witness to this stage of evolution.

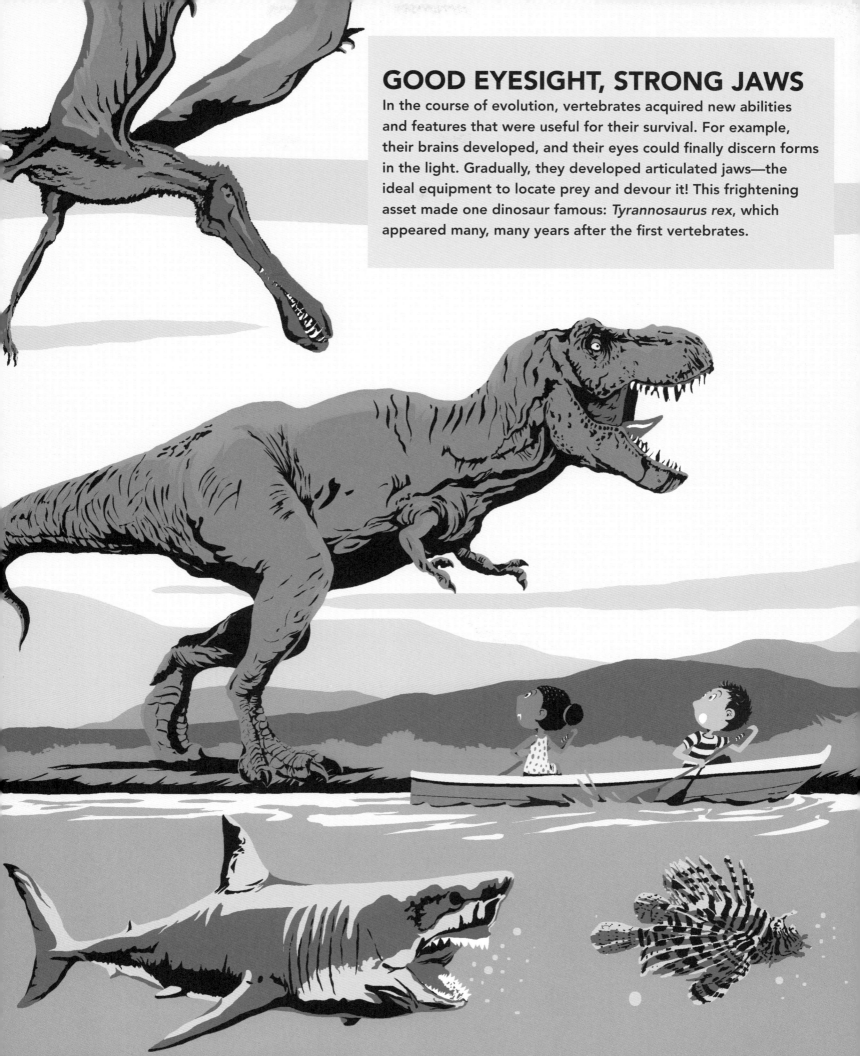

GOOD EYESIGHT, STRONG JAWS

In the course of evolution, vertebrates acquired new abilities and features that were useful for their survival. For example, their brains developed, and their eyes could finally discern forms in the light. Gradually, they developed articulated jaws—the ideal equipment to locate prey and devour it! This frightening asset made one dinosaur famous: *Tyrannosaurus rex*, which appeared many, many years after the first vertebrates.

BONES IN THE WATERS

The skeleton of a shark is made of cartilage, which also made up the skeletons of the first vertebrates. As evolution progressed, this internal framework became bony in many animals. As a result, most fish today have lots of hard, thin bones, which are easily trapped between teeth. Humans, which are the terrestrial cousins of marine vertebrates, also have a rigid and solid internal skeleton.

TETRAPODS AND THE CONQUEST OF DRY LAND

It was nearly 350 million years ago that the first four-legged animals set out to conquer dry land. The fins on these descendants of fish gradually evolved into legs. This group, called tetrapods, is the ancient ancestors of mammals, birds, amphibians, and reptiles.

MUCH-NEEDED AIR

When the first terrestrial vertebrates emerged from the waters, they already had the ability to breathe air from the atmosphere, as do some archaic lineages of fish today. Their lungs, which we have inherited, may have come from ancient aquatic ancestors.

ON ALL FOURS

Tetrapods have four limbs, whether paws, wings, legs, or arms. "Tetra" means "four" in Greek. As for the number of fingers, initially it varied between six and eight per extremity. Pentadactyly (having five fingers), which characterizes humans, appeared in the first reptiles; these are the ancestors of today's mammals as well as reptiles and birds. Some animals have to be happy with fewer fingers: an ostrich has two, and the viper has none!

TOP-OF-THE-LINE EARS

Fish already had an inner ear, which picked up vibrations in the water. Their tetrapod descendants were further equipped with a middle ear. It is is made up of tiny bones that resulted from a transformation of the jawbone. The middle ear was capable of transmitting the vibrations in the air to the eardrum. Today we benefit from this evolutionary development.

WHAT LAID THE FIRST EGG ON DRY LAND?

Reptiles were first to lay their eggs on land. They were able to do so because their eggs had a shell, unlike their ancestors, whose eggs were laid in water. Today's amphibians, such as frogs, lay their eggs in water, and their tadpoles grow there. But as adults, they develop lungs and legs and can live on land.

THE RISE OF MAMMALS

About 200 million years ago, tetrapods that had evolved into mammal-like reptiles developed fur. Then they developed mammary glands, an organ that produces milk to feed offspring. These two evolutions resulted in an explosion of diversification. In some mammals, the brain also made great developmental strides.

Humans and other mammals are descended not from dinosaurs but from animals that are even older: mammal-like reptiles, such as the strange and extinct Cynognathus. It lived more than 200 million years ago!

FUR!

Sixty-six million years ago, a giant asteroid crashed into the Earth. The dust it stirred up darkened the sky, and the ensuing cold spell made most terrestrial animals disappear. Mammals survived thanks to their fur, as did some feathered dinosaurs that are the ancestors of today's birds.

A BIG DISCOVERY FROM A LITTLE FOSSIL

In the late 1900s, the fossil of a small furry animal was discovered in China. It is the oldest known placental mammal, and it lived 125 million years ago. Scientists called it *Eomaia*, a word meaning "first mother."

MARSUPIAL OR PLACENTAL?

Kangaroos and koalas are marsupials: their newborns must complete their development in the mother's pouch. But elephants, cats, and human beings are placental mammals, meaning that they develop inside the mother and are fed via an organ called the placenta. As a result, the baby is born with its vital functions fully operational. Marsupials were once widespread throughout the world but now survive only in South America and Australia.

BRAINS AND MAMMALS

With their more developed brains, mammals acquired a new range of behaviors—from living in a group or playing to digging a burrow or climbing a tree to avoid hungry dinosaurs. Another evolution is that they no longer laid eggs. Instead, their young developed inside their belly, then were fed milk from the mother's breasts. There are only two exceptions: the platypus and the echidna (spiny anteater). The females of both still lay eggs, and milk for their young flows from hairs on the mother's belly.

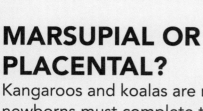

PRIMATES ENTER THE SCENE

Primates appeared 65 million years ago. They include monkey species and humans, as well as their cousins, the tarsiers and lemurs. Primates are the only mammals to have a thumb opposable to their other fingers.

OPPOSABLE THUMBS

Primates are the only mammals that have one finger, the thumb, that is opposable. This means that it can form a pincer with other fingers. It is ideal for grasping a fruit, making a tool, or holding a pencil. The fingers of primates are usually equipped with flat nails, which are good for caressing and delousing—two things that make life in society easier!

A STRONG AND WRINKLED BRAIN

Primates have benefited from many evolutionary changes: improved vision, an enhanced sense of touch, and the ability to live in a society. It is not surprising that their brain, which processes a large amount of information, has grown too.

A primate's brain is much more developed than the brains of other mammals. It also has lots of folds, which increases its surface area. With evolution, intelligence has come to occupy more and more space.

▲

Appearing shortly after the extinction of the dinosaurs 65 million years ago, the now-extinct group called *Purgatorius* is often considered to be the ancestor of primates. These small, rodent-like creatures had flexible ankle bones, making them well adapted to climbing and living in trees.

3-D VISION

Primates have useful hands, and most of them have excellent eyes too. Located on the face (rather than on the side of the skull), their eyes allow them to see in three dimensions. This ability helps them avoid missing their target when jumping from branch to branch. Some primates, such as macaques, baboons, and great apes, also see the world in color.

STANDING TALL

Seven million years ago, great apes, which had already lost their tails, acquired the ability to walk upright. With the arrival of these bipeds, the human lineage was born.

The C-shaped spine of great apes does not allow them to stand for long periods. Their arms are longer, more muscular, and more mobile than ours, and they are well adapted to moving around in trees. Our bipedal ancestors lost that agility millions of years ago!

A GREAT STEP FORWARD

Orangutans, gorillas, gibbons, and chimpanzees are able to walk upright for several feet, but their skeletons are mostly adapted to life in trees. Apes and humans diverged when our ancestors left the forest to live in the savanna. Gradually, they straightened up to walk on two legs, the better to see danger—or dinner—coming.

THE GREAT APES, THAT'S US!

Like other great apes, we do not have a tail but, rather, a coccyx, a series of bones that end the spine. Our skull resembles those of small gorillas. When our ancient cousins become adults, their jaws grow longer and their eyebrow arches thicken, whereas we keep our young great-ape skull all our lives.

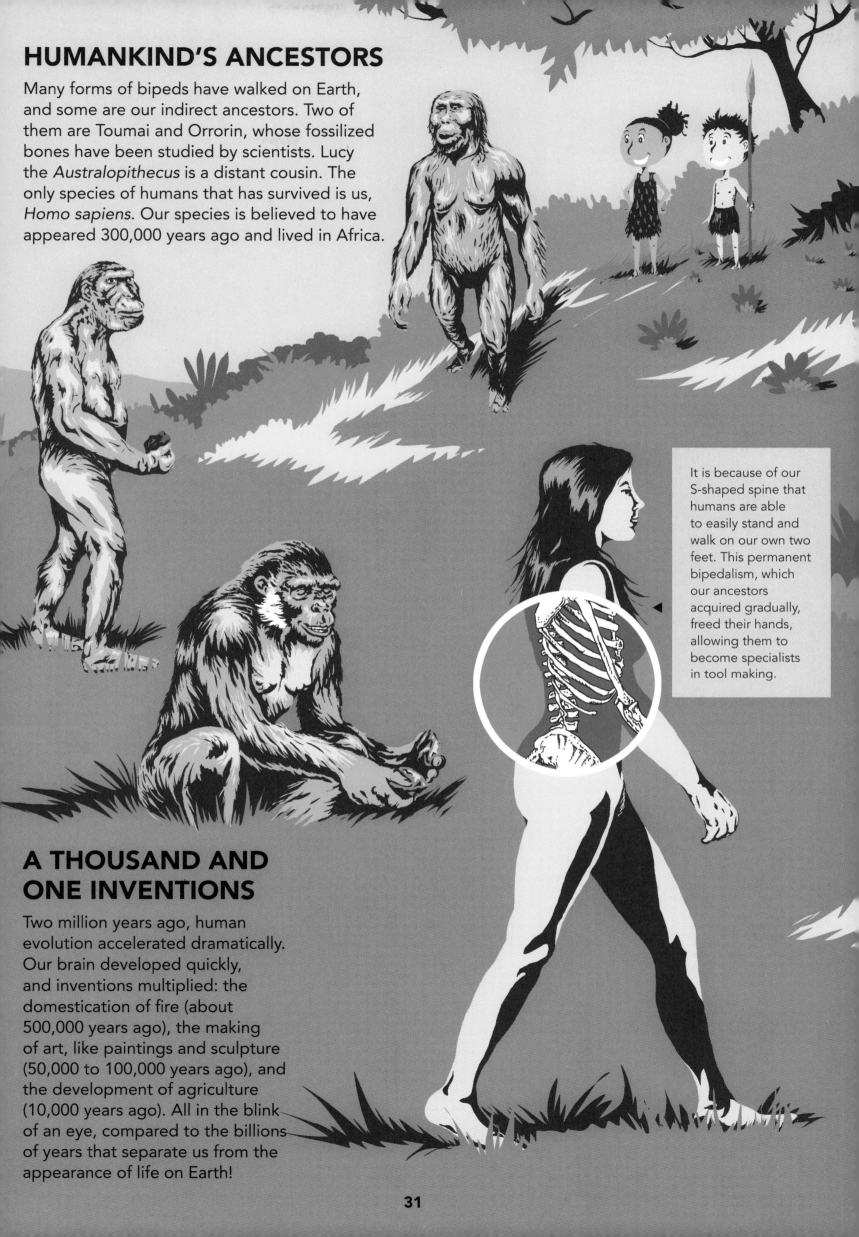

HUMANKIND'S ANCESTORS

Many forms of bipeds have walked on Earth, and some are our indirect ancestors. Two of them are Toumai and Orrorin, whose fossilized bones have been studied by scientists. Lucy the *Australopithecus* is a distant cousin. The only species of humans that has survived is us, *Homo sapiens*. Our species is believed to have appeared 300,000 years ago and lived in Africa.

It is because of our S-shaped spine that humans are able to easily stand and walk on our own two feet. This permanent bipedalism, which our ancestors acquired gradually, freed their hands, allowing them to become specialists in tool making.

A THOUSAND AND ONE INVENTIONS

Two million years ago, human evolution accelerated dramatically. Our brain developed quickly, and inventions multiplied: the domestication of fire (about 500,000 years ago), the making of art, like paintings and sculpture (50,000 to 100,000 years ago), and the development of agriculture (10,000 years ago). All in the blink of an eye, compared to the billions of years that separate us from the appearance of life on Earth!

SPECIES APPEAR AND THEN DISAPPEAR

Like the dinosaurs, millions of animals have disappeared because of natural events, such as cataclysms, diseases, and glaciers. Some have gone extinct because of competition from other species, including us. Today, humans may be the biggest threat to biodiversity, or the variety of life on Earth.

TRILOBITE
Disappeared 250 million years ago

MASS EXTINCTIONS

Sixty-six million years ago, the impact of an asteroid hitting Earth led to the disappearance of dinosaurs and many other animals. But this mass extinction is only one of the five that have taken place since the birth of life. Together they have caused the extinction of 99 percent of species on our planet. The sixth great extinction could be caused by humans. Conserving the wilderness, reducing the waste we produce, saving water—these are just three ways to change our behavior.

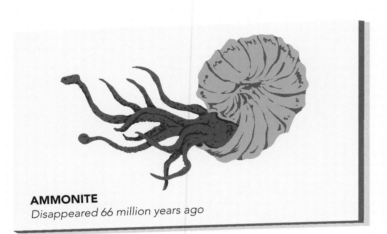

AMMONITE
Disappeared 66 million years ago

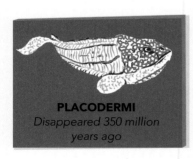

PLACODERMI
Disappeared 350 million years ago

DIPLODOCUS
Disappeared 150 million years ago

SABER-TOOTH TIGER
Disappeared 12,000 years ago

IRISH ELK
*Disappeared
10,000 years ago*

A STEP FORWARD

Other human species have existed at the same time as ours (*Homo sapiens*). "Flores Man" (*Homo floresiensis*; named for an island in Indonesia) was barely more than 3.5 feet tall. This so-called Hobbit became extinct about 50,000 years ago. Before Neanderthals (*Homo neanderthalensis*) disappeared 30,000 years ago, they interbred with *Homo sapiens*. Many of us still carry their genes.

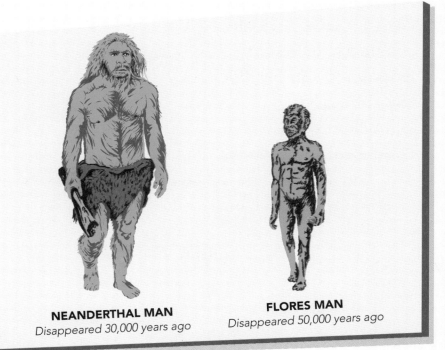

NEANDERTHAL MAN
Disappeared 30,000 years ago

FLORES MAN
Disappeared 50,000 years ago

DODO
Disappeared 340 years ago

GONE BUT NOT FORGOTTEN

The human species, which has no real predator (except itself), is responsible for the extinction of many animals, often by consuming them and polluting or destroying their habitat. Such was the case with the dodo, a flightless bird that lived on the island of Mauritius. The species disappeared completely in the late 1600s because the birds were unable to escape new human settlers and the animals they brought to the island.

▲

The Earth will probably have 12 billion people in 2100, twice as many as in 2000. Year after year, natural resources are diminishing, and the climate is getting warmer. These phenomena threaten the human species. Who knows—planets resembling Earth could one day be home to our descendants. In the meantime, it is urgent to protect our environment and the members of the living world.

THE TREE OF EVOLUTION

This drawing is one way to visualize evolution. From ancestors to cousins to descendants, millions of species have populated the Earth over the past 3.5 billion years.

CRUSTACEANS

INSECTS

ARACHNIDAS

ARTHROPODS

ECHINODERMS

VERTEBRA

MOLLUSKS

CNIDARIA

SPONGES

PLANTS

FUNGI

ANIMALS

EUKARYOTES

CROCODILIAN

ARCHAEA

BACTERIA

VIRUSES

**LUCY
(AUSTRALOPITHECUS)**

**CARTILAGINOUS
FISH**

CHIMPANZEES

BONY FISH

FISH

AMPHIBIANS

**FLORES
MAN**

**GREAT
APES**

TILES

MAMMALS

**NEANDERTHAL
MAN**

PRIMATES

BIRDS

HOMO SAPIENS

OUR TWO HEROES

Here they stand at the end of the great-ape
branch of the evolutionary tree. Other families
are much more diverse. If we were to draw a
branch for each species of insect, for example,
we would need about one million!

GLOSSARY

AMINO ACID This is the molecule that make up proteins in living things.

ARCHAEA We still find ancient microorganisms called archaea near these deep-sea vents.

ARCHAIC A word that describes something that is very old or ancient.

ATOM A microscopic element—which includes oxygen, iron, and sulfur—that is the basic unit of a chemical element.

BACTERIA (singular BACTERIUM) These single-cell microorganisms are found throughout the environment—in the soil, in water, even in your body; some bacteria are harmful, but most are not and many are good.

BIPEDAL An animal that walks on two legs or feet.

CELL A cell is the most fundamental unit of life; these microscopic "building blocks" house DNA and make up all living things.

CNIDARIA This family includes jellyfish, sea anemones, and corals; they were among the first animals.

CYTOPLASM The substances inside a cell's walls but outside the nucleus.

DNA Housed within cells, this molecule is composed of genes that are transmitted from generation to generation. It is DNA that carries heredity.

EUKARYOTIC CELL A highly evolved cell whose DNA is in a nucleus. Assembled together, they make up plants, animals, and most fungi.

EVOLUTION The process of species changing and adapting over time that explains how living things have diversified and developed from earlier forms to usually more complex forms.

FOSSIL The remains or impressions of a once-living thing that are preserved when the skeleton, footprints, dung, or body features have been "mineralized," or turned into rock.

GENE A sequence of DNA that contains specific codes that are useful to living organisms; they allow different substances to be made (proteins, for example).

LINEAGE This biology term is used to identify a group of living beings that have the same common ancestor (for example, the chimpanzee lineage).

MASS EXTINCTION The dying out or disappearance of several different species over a large area in a short time. Several mass extinctions have happened on Earth in the past because of a sudden catastrophic event or environmental change.

MEMBRANE A barrier that protects a cell from the outside environment; it is formed of fat, sugar, and protein.

MITOCHONDRIA Ancient bacteria that act like an energy factory inside eukaryotic cells.

MOLECULE A set of atoms linked together make up a molecule; the materials that surround us and those that compose us are made up of molecules.

MUTATION A change that occurs when a gene is altered, either by chance or because of environmental factors.

NATURAL SELECTION The action of the environment on the survival and reproduction of an individual within a population.

NUCLEUS The command center of a eukaryotic cell that houses the cell's DNA.

PARASITE An organism that needs another living being to survive and reproduce.

PLACENTA A temporary organ that develops during pregnancy in a mammal that nourishes and maintains a fetus via the umbilical cord.

PRIMATE A group of mammals that includes humans, apes, and lemurs.

PROTEIN A molecule made up of amino acids that makes up living things.

REPRODUCE A mechanism that allows a cell or organism to multiply.

SPECIES Apopulation of living beings that can reproduce among themselves and whose descendants are capable of reproducing too.

TETRAPOD The ancient ancestors of mammals, birds, amphibians, and reptiles.

TRANSFOMRATION A term used by Jean-Baptiste de Lamarck at the beginning of the 1800s, before "evolution" became the preferred word.

VERTEBRATE An animal with an internal skeleton or spine that strengthens its body and allows it to perform many movements.

VIRUS A type of germ that causes disease in humans, animals, and plants.